PRESENTS

THE DEFINITIVE GUIDE TO
FORTNITE
2020

A TOTALLY INDEPENDENT PUBLICATION

Written by Naomi Berry
Designed by Chris Dalrymple

A Pillar Box Red Publication

© 2019. Published by Pillar Box Red Publishing Limited. Printed in the EU.

ISBN 978-1-912456-37-6

WELCOME

There's no denying that Fortnite has taken the world by storm (pun most definitely intended).

Since its release, Fortnite has grown beyond its humble beginnings as a more colourful alternative in the battle royale pantheon and has become a true staple of modern popular culture. It's been the game that has united a lot of different people – even if you're not into gaming, you sure know about Fortnite.

So what makes it so special? Its appeal lies in its simplicity – a last man standing scenario with new tricks and whirls added in to keep it fresh. The Fortnite developers are dedicated to keeping the game alive, constantly rebalancing, tinkering and bringing new content to the fore.

But at its core, its long-lasting genius is the game mechanics and its accessibility. You can pick up the game today and train yourself to hold your own against seasoned players. And the new content and updates mean that there's always something new to learn and master, even for those who have been playing since day 1. It's never too late to be the last one standing (well, unless you're X-quadrants deep in a Stage 7 storm, but you get the gist) and when you do get there, there'll be a brand new challenge to face on your next try.

This guide is here to help you master the art of battle royale, so any new curveballs that the game may throw at you will simply glide off your shoulder as you dust them off, non-plussed. So strap in: there's a storm forming.

CONTENTS

GLOSSARY

Fortnite may take place on a tiny little island, but sometimes it feels like a whole nation logging in to take each other down, with its own customs, culture and even communication. It can be a little daunting learning the lingo, especially when it seems like a whole other language at times.

Understanding the terminology is helpful for general game knowledge, but it's borderline integral if you're playing with teammates and want to communicate in the most effective way possible. Here's a quick list of the basic phrases you'll come across that may seem a little alien at first, but will feel as familiar as skydiving into a death pit from a big blue bus held up by a balloon in no time.

BATTLE PASS: A Battle Pass is an in-game purchase that is available every season. Along with new cosmetics, it also provides special challenges and tasks for the player to complete, and rewards their progress with items and V-Bucks.

BLOOM: A weapon's bloom refers to the spray of its bullets once fired. A weapon that has bloom will fire a bullet anywhere within its crosshair, which has lower accuracy than a direct snipe. You can lower the chance of bloom by standing still or crouching while shooting.

THE BUBBLE: The circle of the map that is unaffected by the storm, i.e. the playing area.

BUSH CAMPER: Refers to players that take cover and hide in bushes.

BM: This stands for 'Bad Manners', and is a light take on post-kill or post-win celebrations at the expense of the opponent (like breakdancing on their corpse, for example).

BOT: A term used to refer to players who are playing badly, or making poor game decisions.

DPS: Stands for "Damage Per Second". This is usually used in reference to weapon power.

HEALS: Any item that provides health points, like bandages, medikits, and even campfires.

LAUNCH: The phrase "I have a launch" generally means that they have a launch pad.

LOADOUT: The weaponry and items you have in your arsenal. Having an 'Ideal Loadout' in mind while playing will speed up the loot and subsequent cop-or-drop decision making process.

LTM: Stands for "Limited Time Mode". These are special game modes that developers introduce to spice up gameplay for a season, or a limited event.

KNOCKED: To 'knock' an opponent means to knock them down without fully eliminating them.

MATS: "Mats" is shorthand for materials, i.e. wood, brick and metal.

MINIS: There are a lot of mini-somethings in Fortnite, but the solo 'mini' refers to the "Small Shield Potion".

NO SKIN: A player that does not have a custom skin equipped.

ONE/ONE-SHOT: When an opponent is 'one' or 'one-shot', it means that they are one shot away from being knocked down. This is vital communication for teammates as it can dictate whether they should rush an enemy or take cover.

POI: An acronym for Point of Interest. On the Battle Royale map, POIs are notable locations on the island (like Lazy Lagoon, Fatal Fields, Mega Mall etc.), including unnamed areas (like the Stadium, Viking Village and the Hot Springs).

PVE: An acronym for "Player versus Environment". This is non-online play, and is the game mode in Fortnite: Save the World.

PVP: An acronym for Player versus Player. This is online play, and is the game mode in Fortnite: Battle Royale.

REZ: Shorthand for resurrection, used by players who require teammates to pick them up.

RUSH: To rush an opponent means to make a direct offensive push upon them to kill them. This is a risky move as there's no way to know whether your opponent has healing items or superior weaponry, it's best to execute this when you know your opponent is weak or one-shot.

SHIELD POP: This call means that an opponent's shield has been either partially or fully destroyed.

SPAWN ISLAND: The area you are loaded into while waiting for the game to start. You cannot access this part of the map once the game has begun, but you can see it in the distance from the main island.

TAG/TAGGED: Either dealing a hit or acquiring a hit. If someone is tagged, it means they have been hit. This can let teammates know to either finish off the kill, or help you heal up.

V-BUCKS: Fortnite's in-game currency that can be used to buy custom cosmetic items, including costumes, items and weapon skins, and dance emotes.

THE 3 BASICS:
GATHERING

Gathering is the fundamental basic that is the foundation of your Fortnite experience. Everything you build and craft requires materials that you have to find, forage and utilise all across the map.

In Battle Royale, there are ultimately three rudimentary categories that all materials fall into: wood, stone and metal.

TIP!

Be efficient in your gathering and use the Critical Point. This blue circle marks the weakest point of your target, and hitting it will speed up the gathering process and increase the material yield.

TOOLS OF THE TRADE

You'll start every match with your trusty pickaxe: a key tool for gathering and a last resort weapon in desperate times. This tool is what you need to destroy the world around you to reap your resources. All pickaxes are made equal, but you can jazz yours up with your choice of cosmetic skin.

TIP!

Don't just throw your axe around like a madman. Be sure to check for boxes and chests before you swing; if you strike a box before you inspect it, you'll destroy it without a chance to obtain the items inside.

WOOD

Wood is easily the most abundant of the three resources, and while it is the fastest to build with, it is the least durable, with the least HP of all three materials. So where can you pick up some trusty timber?

›TREES:

This is somewhat of a no-brainer, but trees are the most common source of the material and can be found all over the map.

TIP!

When hacking trees, don't take them down completely; their disappearance animation can alert your enemy to your location from quite some distance. Try just leaving them with a smidge of HP.

›WOODEN BUILDINGS:

Huts and shacks dotted around the map can be broken down for resources.

·FENCES:
These are great to target if you drop in a residential area and need resources quickly, as they break very easily.

·OTHER:
Crates, wooden pallets, boxes, certain pieces of furniture, cacti (surprisingly enough).

STONE
Stone is one step up from wood in terms of durability. Think of it as the middle-man; it's the 2nd fastest to build with and has the 2nd most HP (2nd out of 3, of course). Where can you stock up on stone?

·ROCKS:
These natural resources can be found across the map. Rocks give way more stone than walls and structures, but are harder to find.

·STONE BUILDINGS:
Of course. Most of the structures in town-areas across the map are built from stone. But be warned: they take significantly longer to break down.

·OTHER:
Rubble piles

METAL
Metal is the sturdiest of all the materials but takes the longest time to build with. With great power comes great... wait times? So where can you mine some metal?

› VEHICLES:
This is your highest payout resource, around 30 metal per hit. But be careful! Some cars have alarms, which – if set off – will immediately draw attention to your location.

› IRON FENCES:
Fences have a low payout but are fast to take down, so are good for a quick fix.

› SHIPPING CONTAINERS:
These can be found most commonly in industrial areas.

› OTHER:
Lamp posts, pipes, certain pieces of furniture.

TIP!
You can also find a variety building resources in Supply Drops, Loot Llamas and Chests. Oh, and raiding your victim's supplies after you kill them, of course.

TIP!
Don't be stingy with your harvest. You can hold up to x999 of any resource at a time, and you'll never know when you'll need to use them, so stock up.

THE 3 BASICS:
BUILDING

With your resources in tow, now it's time to put them to use. Building is what sets Fortnite apart from its fellow battle royale titles, but the game's hallmark component certainly isn't simple to utilise. It takes time to truly master building, and this quick guide should set you in right direction as you go from My First Shack to Frank Lloyd Wright whipping out the Guggenheim.

TIP!

Practice building different structures without the pressure of imminent death looming over your shoulder in Creative mode.

WHY BUILD?

The Battle Royale island is already populated with a wide variety and plethora of interesting structures from Scandinavian hamlets to Uncle Pete's Pizza Pit, so why build at all?

You can use structures to create cover, interrupt lines of sight, break your fall from unexpected tumbles, create shortcuts between mountains... And you can edit everything you build as you go to suit your needs. If your arsenal is your attack, then your building materials are your defense, and bear half of the responsibility for keeping you alive.

TIP!

Make sure that Turbo Build is enabled. This allows you to hold down left-click and continually place structures at your aim. You can enable this under the Game Tab in the settings menu.

BUILDING BLOCKS: BUILDING 101

》 All three materials can be used to construct four types of structure: walls, ramps, floors and roofs.

》 The material determines the minimum (start) and maximum HP of the structure.

》 Each individual structure will cost 10 of your material.

》 Remember, while you can use a building for defense, you can also use it offensively to box in opponents.

KNOW YOUR MATERIALS

You learnt where to harvest your resources in the previous pages, but it's equally as important to know the numbers behind each – starting HP, maximum HP, time to reach maximum HP – so you know how durable your structure is and how long you have if you're under attack.

So, in general, wood may be flimsy, but it's fast, and should be used for building in emergencies (avoiding fall damage, escaping an enemy, the last throws of a battle etc.). Metal is better for late-game structures and build battles.

Material	Structure	Min. HP	Max. HP	Secs to Reach Max. HP
Wood	Wall	90	150	4
	Ramp /Floor/Roof	84	140	3.5
Stone	Wall	99	300	11.5
	Ramp /Floor/Roof	93	280	12
Metal	Wall	110	500	24.5
	Ramp /Floor/Roof	101	460	22.5

THE IMPORTANCE OF FOUNDATION

For any structure to stand, it has to be anchored to some point on the map. That means that to topple any structure, it only takes some well-placed shots at the foundations of a build (or one stellar rocket) to take the whole thing down, no matter the height. This is important to keep in mind in a few scenarios:

1. When you're building, it's important to ensure that you have more than one anchor for your structure (see the 'Bread and Butter Structures' section for more details) so your enemy has to take down several targets to topple your build, giving you more time to escape or think of a strategy. Use cliffs and the sides of buildings to provide multiple anchor points.

2. When you're approaching someone that is sniping from high ground, taking down their tower by destroying the foundation is a quick way to even the playing field.

3. Also, if you come across two players engaged in a battle fight, you can easily take out the foundations in order to strike when they're both otherwise distracted. If they haven't already taken each other's HP low enough, the fall damage and surprise at the sudden fall will certainly work in your favour.

EDITING

Even the greatest artists need to take some time to review their work, and building in Fortnite is no different. Hey, Rome wasn't built in a day, and while you don't quite have that luxury of time, you do have a chance to make changes to your structure once it has been built.

› WINDOWS:

Creating a window gives you a vantage point for shooting, and also crouch shooting.

› DOORS:

When an enemy is busy trying to gun down the front of your structure, building a door to sneak out of at the back is a quicker (and less telling) escape than breaking down the wall to leave.

› FLOORS:

You can edit squares of your 4x4 floor to create openings heading down. Use these either to ambush enemies passing below or to make a low-ground escape route.

› PARTIAL WALLS:

You can also remove sections of a wall for the same peek/cover purpose.

BREAD AND BUTTER STRUCTURES

Your imagination is truly the limit when it comes to Fortnite's building system, but here are some basic, bread and butter structures that would be good to familiarize yourself with for maximum gameplay efficiency. Practice these in Creative and you'll be throwing them up in Battle Royale in no time.

TIP!

Don't forget the importance of a good roof over your head. It can be easy to neglect, but they prevent any enemy ambushes from above. They can also be used to box in opponents if you throw a quick trap in there to boot.

› THE 1X1:

This is the most basic of builds — four walls with ramp in the center, and a roof. A 1x1 is your little cube of solace, and can be thrown up to provide quick cover as you formulate your next move, or gather around a campfire to reboot before moving on.

› BASIC RAMP:

A basic ramp is an easy build that yields a lot of benefits. It allows you the advantage of higher ground (either for scoring headshots or getting the drop on an enemy), as well as providing more cover as you peek over the top. If the enemy is busy taking down your ramp, they're not aiming at your head. Aim at theirs.

› REINFORCED RAMP:

This is a step up from the basic ramp in both effort and material costs. As you build the ramp, build walls and floors beneath each incline to provide more structures that your opponent must shoot through in order to topple your build. It means three structures per incline instead of one, but it's three times as sturdy.

› TURTLE:

A turtle is a very simple structure that can be expanded to infinite possibility, but the bigger it becomes, the harder it is to manage. At its base, it's simply a 1x1 with a roof. But placing these next to each other and editing through them allows you extended cover if under fire. These structures have serious defensive power, but you'll need to be quick with editing and repairs to get the most out of it.

› 90s:

90s are the fastest and most advanced build from this list. The name comes from the building process, in which you turn left or right by 90 degrees, building up one floor with each turn. You need to be really familiar with turbo building to pull these off, and they require a lot of practice. The best way to start is to get used to turning, jumping and building simultaneously. Try looking up tutorials on YouTube to further your skills.

In battle, these are best used to get quick vertical distance from your opponent and the chance to get immediate high ground to take your shot from. Realistically, most battles will only call for two or three 90s before attacking; build too high, and you might lose track of them, or worse, be susceptible to fall damage.

TIP!

Change your keybinds to what works for you when it comes to building. Sometimes the default settings aren't always the most intuitive, and you have to be ready to pull off some fast fingered inputs to build some of these structures when under fire.

THE 3 BASICS:
SURVIVING - WEAPONS

When it comes down to it, Fortnite is a Battle Royale game, and while it may be a nice notion that you just kind of hope the enclosing storm will take care of the other 99 people on that island with you, you're going to have to take matters into your own hands and rack up that kill count if you want to be the last one standing. That's where weapons come in.

The weaponry in Fortnite seems to change as often as the sun sets, so it's impossible to keep full track of what's in, what's out, what's still OP and what's been vaulted, but regardless of what comes and goes (peace out, Boom Bow, you won't be missed), every weapon falls under a certain category of type, rarity and ammo.

RARITIES

HERE TODAY, GONE TOMORROW

Not every weapon introduced to Fortnite stands the test of time. Each season retires a few select pieces of weaponry into the Vault (usually for the sake of the game's balance). But don't count out a comeback: the developers have been known to crack open the Vault and put old weapons back into rotation in new updates or LTMs.

Like all items and cosmetics in Fortnite, weapons go by a rarity hierarchy that dictates how easy (or difficult) it will be to find it in game, and, of course, how powerful its performance will be. All rarity is colour-coded, and is related as follows:

Common (grey)
Uncommon (green)
Rare (blue)
Epic (purple)
Legendary (orange)

While generally, the higher the rarity, the better the weapon, it is important to remember that ranking isn't everything. You shouldn't simply toss a green weapon because you found an Epic; be smart with your picks and carry weapons that you are comfortable with using and provide a variety of versatility when it comes to combat.

FINDING HIGH TIER WEAPONS

While there does seem to be an ample amount of things scattered down there, it's unlikely you're going to find an Epic or Legendary weapon just lying on the ground. You'll need to put in a little more effort to find and wield these guys, but luckily, you now know just where to look:

▶ **Treasure Chests:** Listen out for that distinctive hum and you might just find yourself a high-tier weapon in one of those trusty golden chests.

▶ **Supply Boxes:** Keep an eye on the skies for balloons and on the ground for blue smoke to find out where Supply Boxes are going to land. Be careful when rushing to collect the loot though; you're unlikely to be the only player to have spotted its fall.

▶ **Vending Machines:** You can trade in materials for Rare or higher weapons if you come across one of the several vending machines scattered across the map. Their colours indicate what rarity of item they contain, and they will disappear once the item has been claimed.

AMMO

Ammo is required for all weapons, excluding explosive and melee types. Each weapon type fires a specific type of ammo, which vary in rarity.

Ammo Type	Rarity	Weapon
Light Bullets	Uncommon	Pistols, SMGs
Medium Bullets	Uncommon	Assault Rifles
Heavy Bullets	Uncommon	Sniper Rifles
Shells	Uncommon	Shotguns
Rockets	Common	Grenade Launchers, Rocket Launchers

WEAPON TYPES

ASSAULT RIFLES

Assault rifles are pretty versatile guns in that they work well across all ranges, have a high damage output and a reasonably high fire rate. This versatility makes them great weapons for beginners who aren't as familiar with shooting mechanics. Just aim and shoot: simple.

WEAPON TIPS:

❯ Assault rifles have a pretty unfortunate bloom, so try to shoot in small bursts in order to retain accuracy and suppress the recoil.

❯ With the above in mind, you can afford to spam shots close range, but should practice smaller bursts at medium range, and single shots at long.

❯ These guns (like the vast majority of the Fortnite arsenal) are hitscan, which means the shot connects as soon as you pull the trigger (i.e., no bullet travel time). Keep your crossfire on your target and practice your tracking to take down an enemy in a few shots.

SUB MACHINE GUNS (SMGS)

SMGs have an incredibly high fire rate. Their impressive DPS is balanced out by a high damage drop-off and high spread limiting their optimum range. Up close, these are deadly; anything further than mid-range, they're pretty ineffective.

WEAPON TIPS:

❯ Due to the rapid fire rate, SMGs can eat up a lot of ammo without you realising, so try to use controlled bursts to keep on top of your ammo count.

❯ If you're attacking an opponent far away, close the distance with another weapon before switching to the SMG to finish things off at close quarters.

❯ Don't rely solely on your SMG; it works best as a companion weapon, used in tandem with Shotguns or Rifles.

SHOTGUNS

Like SMGs, shotguns are most effective at close-range, and while they both deal a lot of damage to opponents, shotguns inflict it faster. Each shotgun blast is comprised of numerous pellets, and the shot's damage is calculated based on how many of those pellets hit your target (shown by the red dots in your crosshair post-shot).

WEAPON TIPS:

❱ Shotguns are slow to fire, but definitely worth the slot in your loadout, as their close range damage makes them perfect for 1v1 duels. Aim for the head!

❱ These are a dueling weapon. You should practice building between each shot to ensure you have both good offense and defense.

❱ Shotguns are terrible for destroying builds, so switch to another weapon to attack structures. Don't waste your ammo.

MINIGUNS

Miniguns have a very fast rate of fire and don't require a reload, and while they're ideal for tearing through both people and structures alike, unfortunately their extremely loud noise practically gives any lurking opponent your direct coordinates.

WEAPON TIPS:

❱ Miniguns take a little time to get their barrels spinning before firing, so take that into account before you launch into an engagement.

❱ Relentless shots sacrifice accuracy, so don't try using these at a distance.

PISTOLS

The pistol category covers a wide range of weapons of all shapes and sizes, with different ranges, rarity, damage and accuracy. While these may not be anyone's number one pick, they're a great backup weapon to have, and your choice of pistol should depend on the other weapons' ranges in your loadout. Due to their variety, it's important to be familiar with the different pistol types, so pop into Creative and get to know what you're shooting.

WEAPON TIPS:

⟩ Generally, pistols have an average to high damage, and their damage drop off means they are most effective at short to mid range.

⟩ Pistols can be used in very effective weapon combos, particularly with burst damage guns. Start a fight with a Pistol and switch to an SMG or Shotgun to finish.

SNIPER RIFLES

These guns are not for the rookies, and rely on the players' ability to track their enemy and consider bullet travel time. Yep, rifles are not hitscan, which means that when a rifle fires, the bullet does not immediately connect with the target as it does with other guns. Bullet travel time means you have to predict your enemy's movements if they are not still.

While they are definitely the most skillfully demanding of guns, their long range makes them great for sniping unsuspecting enemies from afar, and some variants even have the ability to one-shot kill.

WEAPON TIPS:

⟩ As sniper rifles are very slow to fire, you have to be prepared to switch to another weapon immediately after firing.

⟩ When you're lining up your shot, keep in mind that you won't be the only player on the map with a sniper in their loadout. Take (or make) cover, and be efficient with your time when lining up your shots. You don't want to be a sitting duck.

⟩ Practice. Practice, practice, practice. They say it makes perfect, you know.

LAUNCHERS

Rockets: for those times where bullets just aren't getting the job done. Launchers deal a huge amount of damage to players and structures, as they have both direct hit and splash damage. Of course, such mammoth damage capability comes with a trade-off, in that launchers are both slow to fire and the shots take some time to reach the target.

WEAPON TIPS:

❱ Use a launcher to deal damage to groups of enemies with a single shot.

❱ Launchers are great weapons to quickly topple an enemy's structure by firing at its foundations.

❱ Splash damage is a double-edged sword in that it may deal damage to surrounding enemies, but it can also deal that same damage to you, should you be in range. Your teammates, however, are immune.

OTHERS

Fortnite is a game where you can hunt down your enemies dressed in a Black Ops bodysuit or as a giant banana, so of course Epic has thrown in some more... "unorthodox" weaponry amongst the more traditional guns to choose from.

Depending on the patch, these can vary from a deadly crossbow, a bomb that makes your enemies break into dance, a bottle that summons a storm, or even Captain America's shield. Each season comes with new goodies to replace the ones that have been vaulted; just remember you can try them out any time in Creative mode.

THE 3 BASICS:
SURVIVING - WINNING THE 1V1

SETTINGS FOR SURVIVAL

Before you even think about jumping into a one-on-one, it's important that you customise your in-game settings to whatever is most comfortable for you. This seems like a nitty-gritty detail that is often overlooked, but any player worth their salt will customise play settings first in any competitive PVP game.

That's not to say that this guide is going to tell you exactly what numbers to input, for the same reason there's no point in incessantly spamming a pro player's Twitch chat for their settings: everyone operates differently, and you need to find what works for your playstyle and your hardware, not for anyone else.

If you're on a PC, be sure to adjust your mouse and gamepad sensitivities, and your mouse DPI. Console players need to adjust the Gamepad ADS and Scope sensitivities. Fiddle around until you find a fit that is comfortable. You might need to trial and error a few set-ups before you find the best one for you.

YOUR LOADOUT

Your loadout is yours to customise however you see fit, but there's a general balance you should keep in mind if you want the most optimal hotbar: two slots for weapons (with one reserved for an Assault Rifle), two for health and shields, and the last is dealer's choice. This is a good defensive set-up, which allows you to play more on the safe side as you get to know the ropes. Once you're more comfortable with battles and building, you may be better suited to a four weapon/one heal item loadout.

THINK BEFORE YOU SHOOT

You know, they say you win 100% of the fights that you don't risk losing... Or something? Basically, you don't need to take on every fight, and a key skill to develop is to stop and think before you charge in: what is my risk of loss for this fight?

'Assessment' is the word for the wise. Not every opponent you spot needs to be engaged with upon first sight. Take a pause for a moment. You don't know what loadout they have, but you do know yours. Are you properly equipped for the kind of fight that will incur if you engage? It may be better for you to lay low and sleuth to wait until they're vulnerable, or sneak away to heal up or find some weapons better suited to the scenario.

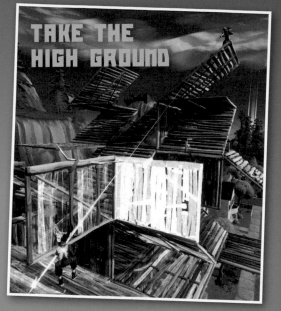

TAKE THE HIGH GROUND

There's a golden rule in any game that involves a gun and aim: high ground is paramount. The map won't always help you out in every scenario, so you'll often have to rely on your building skills to get the height advantage. Practice the Bread and Butter structures listed in 'The 3 Basics: Building' – particularly the reinforced ramp and the 90s – to get comfortable with the mechanics. The faster you can build, the quicker you will get the high ground advantage.

TIP!

Always keep your eye on your opponent while building.

TIP!

When breaking an opponent's structure, shoot down both the foundation and a higher point in the build. This will create two points of destruction, giving the enemy less time to prepare for the fall.

JUMP, JUMP, JUMP

Need it be said again? Jumping may decrease your accuracy, but it increases your survival odds. While accuracy may not be something you'd be quick to sacrifice, it's actually pretty easy to work your way around that disadvantage while jumping, provided you're prepared in advance. That's what we're here for. You're welcome.

Keep in mind that when you jump, your weapon bloom will increase (i.e., your aim accuracy will drop). While that may rule out any jumping snipe-shots from across the map, you will find yourself in situations where accuracy isn't all that important (i.e., super up close and personal with a shotgun, or breaking down an enemy structure.) Keep jumping; it makes you an unpredictable target, and harder to hit.

HEALTH AND SHIELDS

It's not enough just to shoot your way to victory in Battle Royale; a huge part of earning a Victory Royale in Fortnite is bouncing back from fights, recovering from scuffles and keeping yourself healthy enough to last to the very end. Your health and shields are just as integral to surviving the round as your aim, and should always be prioritised.

Keep an eye on your health when roaming around. The green bar represents your health points (HP), and the blue bar represents your shield, which protects your health and depletes before any of your HP when taking damage. If your health bar reaches 0, you'll either be knocked out or eliminated, so always be on the lookout for items you can use to keep yourself topped up and fighting fit. You know what they say: a shield potion a day keeps the kill drone away.

RESTORING SHIELDS

SMALL SHIELD POTIONS (UNCOMMON)

Small Shield Potions can restore 25 shield points, but cannot be used if your shield is more than 50. However, they only take 2 seconds to use and you can carry up to 10 in one slot, so they're a useful band-aid fix in a pinch.

SHIELD POTIONS (RARE)

Shield Potions are a little more substantial than their smaller version and restore 50 shield points. They take 5 seconds to use, can fully restore your shields if stacked, and you can carry a maximum of 2 in one slot.

RESTORING HEALTH

HEALING TIP!

When it comes to healing, prioritise using smaller items first. They may be less effective but the lower cast time will give you small bursts of health that you'll need to survive if an enemy breaks your cover before you can fully heal. Only risk using heavy duty items when you're 100% certain that you're alone, or you have enough materials to build fortifications around yourself before using them.

MUSHROOMS

Mushrooms serve as a super quick fix to an ailing shield should you be lucky enough to find them growing on the ground. These glittering blue veggies restore 5 shield points when eaten, and spawn randomly across the map (usually in shady grass areas, beneath the trees). 5 may seem meagre, but they have no cap, so you can munch on mushrooms all the way to a fully restored shield, if you find enough.

BANDAGES (COMMON)

Bandages should be the bread and butter of your recovery kit, and heal 15 health points when used. They only take 4 seconds to use, but they have their restrictions: they can only heal up to 75 HP, and you can only store a maximum of 15 in one slot.

MEDKITS (UNCOMMON)

Medkits are much more potent and can heal up to 100 HP. However, they're a risky use as they take 10 seconds to use, so ensure that you have taken cover before cracking one out. You can store a maximum of 3 Medkits in one slot.

GETTING YOUR FIVE A DAY

While apples have always been a go-to for a foraged health fix, the developers have since introduced a bunch of new consumable fruits and vegetables that the player can find across the Battle Royale map for a quick pick-me-up. While not quite as effective as Bandages or Medkits, they do still offer different benefits to the player.

CAMPFIRES (RARE)

If you're playing duo, in a team or feeling particularly secure in solo, setting up a campfire is a good way to restore depleted health. Campfires are different than the other items listed in that they are classified as Traps, not items. Place one on the ground and it will heal 50 health points per 2 seconds for a 25 second duration. You can even throw out two and wedge yourself between them for double the healing. But be careful, campfires will heal anyone around them – even enemies.

You can find Cozy Campfires in treasure chests, and Environmental Campfires across the map.

COCONUTS

Coconuts grant 5 effective health points (they'll also regenerate shields if the player is at max health). They can be found in both tropical and desert biomes. If you see a palm tree, give it a whack with your pickaxe: a coconut will likely drop down for your efforts. The Oasis (near the Truck'N'Oasis) is lined with several palm trees, but be careful that the coconuts don't fall into the water when you whack the trunks.

PEPPERS

Peppers grant 5 health points and give a 20% boost to your movement speed for 10 seconds. They can be discovered on the ground in green grassy areas of the desert biome. Look towards the center of Paradise Palms.

APPLES

Apples are the OG foraged consumable. They grant 5 health points when eaten, and usually spawn in clusters, so they can be easy to spot if you know where to look. They can be found on the ground under trees in areas like Loot Lake, Dusty Divot, Salty Springs and Fatal Fields.

BANANAS

Like apples, bananas grant 5 health points when consumed. They can be found exclusively in the tropical biome. Be sure to keep an eye out around small trees with large leaves to spot any bananas on the ground.

DOUBLE DUTY

There are some items that restore both health and shields. Slurp Juice will heal 75 HP over a period of 150 seconds, and will restore your shields when your health is full. You can also find the legendary Chug Jug, which fully restores both your health and shields, but takes a full 15 seconds to drink. Swig at your own peril.

THE HEALING HIERARCHY

While all restorative items are certainly welcomed, unfortunately the inventory is not unlimited, and space constraints force you to pick one over the other. When it comes to potency, keep this hierarchy in mind:

Bandages < Medkit < Small Shield Potion < Slurp Juice < Shield Potion < Chug Jug

If you're playing smartly, you should be focusing on keeping your shields up so you don't have to worry about carrying items to restore your health.

Of course, this doesn't mean you should totally forgo Bandages; you'll need them for burst healing in close encounters with the enemy, or for when you're trying to escape from within the storm. Just be ready to toss them to make space for the elusive Chug Jug, should you be fortunate enough to find one.

REMEMBER!

Shields don't protect you from storm or fall damage! Nope, that hurt comes straight out of your health points. Keep that in mind when making any quick escapes.

PRO GAMER FORTNITE

PRO SURVIVAL TIPS

So you've memorised your key terms, covered the three basics, and learned how to get the advantage in a 1v1... Before you jump off of that Battle Bus and launch into the world of vehicles, choosing landing locations and making your way around the map, it's time to brush up on a few little tricks and tips to ensure you'll be the last one standing.

THE STORM

▶ Never forget the storm! It sounds silly to state, but it's very easy to get so caught up in the PVP duels and takedowns that you forget there's also a PVE element shrinking in on you the whole time. The storm does even more damage during the later stages of the game, so don't be acting too foolhardy if you get stuck in the purple.

▶ Don't relax when you reach the safe zone; remember that a lot of other players will have also outrun the storm and will just be arriving in the peripherals of the eye i.e., where you're likely standing. Players will be flooding from the outside in, so keep this in mind to avoid getting shot in the back.

▶ You can also flip the above knowledge to develop an assault strategy. If you're in the safe zone of the storm, head to edges, take cover, and look to pick off any approaching players that are running in.

SOUNDS

▶ Try to limit the noise you make to keep your cover. Running is a very loud action, so opt for walking and crouching for a less audibly-detectable approach.

▶ If you can, play with headphones rather than device speakers. You'd be surprised at the audio detail (like an enemy's approaching footsteps from a distance) that you might be missing.

SPOTTING ENEMIES

❱ Keep an eye out for open doors, broken walls, empty/open lootboxes and player-built structures.

❱ Keep an ear out for footsteps and the swing of the pickaxe. There's also a special sound cue when an enemy switches their weapon (there's actually a subtle difference in the sound depending on the weapon type, so if you listen really carefully, you can get the heads up on what they're armed with and decide how to respond more quickly.)

CONSERVE AND CAUTION

❱ Were you raised in a barn? Close the door behind you when you head into a structure. This will both cover your tracks and allow you to hear when other intruders enter; your very own little security system.

❱ Keep cover as much as you possibly can while moving. Avoid running across open areas, because you never know who is perched on a distant cliff, sniper rifle at the ready.

❱ It may be tempting to loot an enemy you just shot down, but resist the urge to do so until you've had a good scout. Engagements generally create a lot of commotion, and there's a good chance you've drawn at least one player's attention with that skerfuffle.

❱ Looting renders you super vulnerable: you're a static target, more focused on your loadout than your surroundings. Build around yourself for some quick cover while pilfering...

❱ ...Or if you suspect that someone is nearby, you can leave the loot out as a bait to lure in an unsuspecting enemy and snipe them. Remember! Someone could do the same to you, so beware of abandoned piles of loot on the ground!

❱ Bullets leave air tracks, which means you should be able to tell the direction the shooter is in from their shot's trail. Conversely, other players can deduce the same from you, so don't stay in the same area if you whiff a couple of long-range headshots.

STICKING THE LANDING

THE ISLAND

While other games in the genre design new maps every update, Fortnite has dropped players in the same location from Day 1. The Battle Royale island map may have changed over the years (seen a few meteors, emerging biomes, Viking raids etc.; the same of any geographic location, really), but at its roots it has remained the same place, which means players can get really familiar with their battleground, and use that knowledge as an integral part of their battle strategy. If you haven't already, it's time to get to know the island...

UNDERSTANDING BIOMES

Once upon a time, the island was a mass of green... until update 2.2.0 brought biomes, introducing the ever-changing topography of the map we know and love today. Desert, snow, swamps... The biomes are largely just there to provide some alternative scenery on your hunt, but they can have an effect on your likelihood to find things like foraged consumables. Check out 'Getting Five a Day' to read more about what you're more likely to find in which biome.

PRO
GAMER
FORTNITE

KNOW YOUR HOT DROPS

Hot Drop is an area that is a popular pick for players to land in. Generally, areas around the start or directly beneath the Battle Bus route are Hot Drops, as well as central, loot-rich areas like Tilted Towers/Neo Tilted, Salty Springs and Retail Row. You can expect a lot of early skirmishes here, so avoid them; or dive right in, if you prefer the challenge.

HAS THAT ALWAYS BEEN THERE?

Your focus may be on the 99 other players on the island, but keep an eye out for anything peculiar or out of the ordinary on the map as you play. Epic Games love to tease updates or new features with hints across the map, like destroying Tilted Towers in Season 8, the meteor shower of Season 4, or the disappearance of the Durr Burger statue.

29

STICKING THE LANDING

Battle Royale isn't just about your aiming skills; it's a race to be the last one standing, and it starts as soon as you leap from that Battle Bus to the island below. Your strategy to win better start from your first second of freefall, or you'll be picked off before you get a chance to whip out that Orange Justice emote you'd been saving all your V-bucks for.

Speed is of the essence – if you just glide on down automatically, all the best loot will be lifted by those who managed to touchdown before you. But to truly master the landing, speed has to be combined with precision: it's all about how to make the fastest landing, and where to make the fastest landing.

LEAPING FROM THE BATTLE BUS

The race begins as soon as you leap from that Battle Bus. There are a ton of micro-decisions that go into your landing, so read up on these and keep them in mind as you start your freefall.

THE WHERE...

❭ Pay attention to the Battle Bus trajectory. Your Golden Rule that shouldn't even need to be uttered into the universe at minimal-decibel whisper (but we'll put it in print anyway) is never land anywhere in the direct route of the bus. Never. Ever, ever, ever. The route changes every game, so check the map for the trajectory as soon as you hit the lobby to pick your drop location ahead of time.

Keep an eye on other players. Most eliminations happen upon landing when everyone's trying to clear out their zone, so landing in a heavily populated area is a sure way to have a very fast round. Avoid this by going for a more sparsely populated area. If you're playing solo, try to get your distance from the Battle Bus route by heading towards the locations on the outskirts of the island. Teams can afford to land more central.

TIP!

Though it might seem safe to land near a singular building or shack in an unnamed area, you have to remember that you're trading solitude for resources. There will be an odd weapon and bandage on the ground, sure, but your arsenal will be much more prepared and a lot quicker if you risk landing in the larger, named locations.

**When you've picked your spot, change your mindset from 'Where' to 'How'...

LANDING TIP 1:

If you want to speed up your landing when you're using your glider, strafe from left to right to hit the ground faster.

LANDING TIP 2:

When your glider has been deployed, point the camera at the ground and press forward. This pushes your glider to quicken your descent.

THE HOW...

Aim for low terrain. This is your first and most basic rule to follow on landing. You start your leap in a sky dive, but your glider will auto-deploy when the player is a certain distance from the ground beneath them. That means above a mountain, your glider will pop out a lot sooner than it would if you were aiming for something low like roads, rivers or ravines. Skydiving is faster than gliding, so you want to aim for lower ground to maximise dive time and delay glider deployment.

Aim for heights. That may sound counter-intuitive to the first point, but it's important to switch your mindset to 'height' when your glider has already auto-deployed. It's better to land on a roof than it is the middle of the street; roofs can be cut down and harvested for materials, and often have chests, weapons and other nifty pickups hidden in the attic. Plus, it's much better to have the high-ground advantage against other players that may have landed in the same area.

Find your angle. It may be tempting to drop out of the bus as close to your selected area as possible, but it's better to deploy in advance and approach your drop spot at an angle. Coming in at an angle is faster than floating directly downwards.

TOUCHDOWN!

Don't spend too much time celebrating how perfectly you nailed that landing; you've got a job to do! Your priority when you land should be the following: loot, loot, a little more loot, and of course, loot.

Prioritise finding a close-range weapon like a shotgun so you can continue your looting trip knowing you can defend yourself should someone challenge you. Once you've loaded up with at least one mid or long range weapon and some Shield Potions (which you should drink immediately) and bandages, you're ready to forage out and start your quest to outrun the storm and kill everyone you see on the way.

MOBILITY: MOVING AROUND THE MAP

You may jump off the Battle Bus and hit the ground running, but you don't have to stick to traveling on foot. There are plenty of other ways to boost your mobility and zip, glide, float and warp across the map for maximum efficiency.

ZIPLINE PRO-TIP

If you're aiming at enemies while zipping, use a hitscan weapon (Assault Rifles and Handguns); they're easier to use when moving.

Zip around the map with ziplines, a static mode of transportation that can give your mobility a quick boost. You can find ziplines all across the map; each biome has around 2 or 3 for you to use. While they're easy enough to use, there are a few things you should keep in mind so you don't become a sitting duck.

SCOUT AND SHOOT

Other than the speed boost, ziplines are also a great vantage point for scoping out the area and spotting enemies. Players can rotate 360 degrees and have full access to their arsenal while riding, so you can toss a grenade or snipe out a lurking competitor.

BE UNPREDICTABLE

If an enemy spots you zipping above them, you have to be unpredictable to avoid being an easy target. Jump off at a random point before the end to disrupt your predicted movement trajectory.

DON'T BE AFRAID TO FALL

Don't be afraid to drop suddenly to avoid an enemy; when using ziplines, players are exempt from fall damage, no matter the height. A quick drop and land won't affect your health, but hanging around in the air as an open target certainly will.

PRO
GAMER
FORTNITE

BALLOONS

30 | 648

RIFT-TO-GO

Up, up and away! Balloons provide a vertical mobility boost that allows players to reach high ground, infiltrate enemy towers and get a stealth air-approach on unaware enemies. These items can be found as floor loot, in chests, supply drops, llamas and vending machines.

UP AND AT 'EM

Balloons come in packs of 20, but you only need 5 to float into the air. 6 is the magic number to get the maximum lift. Inflate the balloons with the primary fire button and let go of the balloons with the secondary fire once you reach your desired height.

BREAK YOUR FALL

Balloons can also be used to soften your landing and lessen fall damage. You can even nullify fall damage, depending on how high you are and how many balloons you have.

Rift-To-Gos were introduced in Season 5. They allow players to create a rift that will teleport them into the sky and activate their glider. Once deployed, rifts remain active for 10 seconds. They can be great to escape the storm or make a hasty retreat.

TRAVEL BUDDIES

Once a rift is made, anyone can follow you through it; both friends and foes. If you're using one to escape a close encounter, be careful that your enemy isn't still on your tail when you warp through.

OUT WITH A BANG

While handy, using rifts creates a loud sound effect that will alert players to your location. It isn't advised to use one in highly populated areas, unless you're in a truly sticky situation.

Fall Height	Balloons Needed to Nullify Fall Damage
3 Stories	0
6 Stories	1
8 Stories	2
8+ Stories	3

GLIDERS

Gliders are a transport item that allow players to soar through the skies. They can save you from fall damage should you take an unexpected tumble, and they can also be used for some faster-than-on-foot movement across the map should you get the opportunity to catch enough air for it to deploy.

Auto Save: For the most part, gliders deploy automatically once your free fall reaches a specific height in relation to the ground. That means your trusty glider has your back if you get too overzealous during a building shoot-out and accidentally back off of a cliff. Hey, it happens to the best of us.

Gliding Pacifist: When using gliders, you cannot use any weapons, or any other items. Think carefully before setting sail; once you've deployed, you will be locked out of any action until you hit the ground.

WHEN TO USE YOUR GLIDER

❯ **From the Battle Bus:** This is the most immediate use of your glider. As soon as you leap from the Battle Bus, you can use your glider to select where you want to land. For the first portion of your fall, you can alternate between gliding and sky diving for speed, but once you reach a certain height, your glider will auto-deploy and you will be locked in.

❯ **From a Launch Pad:** Jump on a launch pad to automatically deploy your glider. You can be strategic in where you place your pad – the greater the height, the longer the glide.

❯ **From a Rift:** Leaping through a rift teleports you directly into the sky, which is prime place for a good glide. Open up your glider when you appear on the other side to make the most of the sudden air travel.

CUSTOMISE YOUR GLIDER

Fortnite is a flex game and your glider is not exempt. There are countless glider skins to choose from, that can be either purchased or unlocked from the Item Shop, completing challenges or ranking up Battle Tiers. These skins are purely cosmetic, and don't provide any gameplay advantages... other than style points.

I'M MARY POPPINS Y'ALL!

If you win a Solo, Duo or Squad Battle Royale, you can unlock a special glider skin: the umbrella! The umbrella is exclusive to BR victors, and allows you to dust off your best Yondu impression when you glide on down to the ground.

❱ **Avoiding the Storm:** Sometimes it's easy to get caught up in the foraging or fighting so long that you don't even notice the giant blue storm edging its way towards you. If the storm edge gets too close for comfort, a glider is a great way to make a head start on your escape, as you can cover ground much faster in air than on foot.

❱ **Creating Some Space:** The glider is also a great tool to put some quick space between you and whoever's hot on your tail. They might have better weapons, but if you have a better inventory, you can avoid the battle altogether. Chuck down a launch pad and glide on out of any hairy situation straight to safety.

❱ **Glide and Scout:** The glider can be a great help if the storm eye has closed in, you're in the last stages of Battle Royale and you can't quite see where those final enemies are hiding. It's a risk to take since using a glider will obviously make you more visible, but it's a good tool to use to scout if searches on foot are coming up moot.

HITCHING A RIDE

Now you know your way around the map, it's a case of working out how to get there. Ziplines and rifts are cute for minor jaunts, but this is a game of urgency. There are enemies chasing you down, teammates somehow stranded a perplexing distance away and a purple storm nipping at your ankles the whole time. Sometimes, when you need to get from Pleasant Park to Fatal Fields pronto, going on foot just won't cut it.

That's where vehicles come in. Vehicles are a reasonably recent addition to the world of Battle Royale (first introduced back in Season 5) and are key to getting from one location to the other at maximum speed.

BALLERS

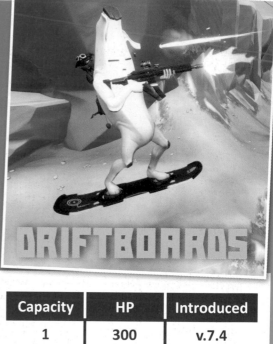

DRIFTBOARDS

Capacity	HP	Introduced
1	150	v.8.1

Capacity	HP	Introduced
1	300	v.7.4

Roll deep with the Baller, a gyroball vehicle that you can hop in and speed your way across the map like your childhood hamster. Ballers are also great for reaching high terrains thanks to its built-in grapple. Just shoot and swing, and you'll be up in the air in no time. Take that, gravity!

Ballers are most commonly found in pirate camps and expedition outposts. It's important to remember that while they can be super speedy, they're not indestructible. With half the HP they were originally introduced with, Ballers can only take 150 damage before they fall apart. Also, players cannot use any weapons or items when inside the gyroball.

The driftboard is a ground vehicle that was released as part of the Driftin' LTM. Since then, it has been available in all game modes and can be found in various locations across the island. If you're not too busy escaping shoot-outs or outrunning lethal storms, you can pull off some tricks like the G-Flip and 18 Orbit and get scored.

This armored hoverboard has a major advantage over the rest of the vehicles in that you can still use weapons and consumables while on board. You can also revive your teammates without having to get off, and it has the added bonus of being particularly quiet in comparison to other vehicles.

QUADCRASHERS

PIRATE CANNON

Capacity	HP	Introduced
2	800	v.8.0

Look, it's not quite a traditional 'vehicle', but it's a mobility item, and it's got four wheels (which has to count for something, right?). The pirate cannon doubles as a weapon and vehicle in that you can either shoot a cannonball from it, or… well, yourself or a friend.

If you go for the latter, then know that once you've been fired, you will be put in a spinning state with no control over the travel trajectory; you'll stop once you spin for about 10 seconds, or, alternatively, collide with something. It can be found at the Lazy Lagoon or at the pirate camps around the map.

Capacity	HP	Introduced
2	400	v.6.1

The quadcrasher lives and dies by its boost, charging it up as soon as someone sits in the driver's seat. A little more duo-friendly than other vehicles, you can saddle up a teammate to join you as you activate boost and smash through almost anything on the map.

Don't limit your four-wheeled wrecking ball fantasies to just structures; you can plough that battering ram bumper into enemies to send them flying into the air too (hello, incoming fall damage). The quadcrasher can also be used to make quick work of mountainous terrains, or catch air via ramps and cliffs.

WHEELED ANTIQUES

The current roster of available vehicles is a lot smaller than what was once on offer. Once upon a time, players could zoom around the map in Attack Terrain Karts (ATKs), shopping trolleys, and even soar across the skies in the much-hated and arguably OP X-4 Stormwing planes. These vehicles have currently been placed in the Vault, but who knows if the developers feel like dusting them out again for a future season?

QUIZ - HOW LONG WILL YOU SURVIVE?

So we've come to this point: you've read up on all of our tips and tricks, now it's time to put it to practice. But before you leap out of the Battle Bus, why not take a quick quiz and see how long you'd last, hypothetically speaking? Take the test and check your answers and results on p. 62-63!

1. What type of ammo do Assault Rifles require?

A. Light

B. Medium

C. Heavy

D. Shells

4. What's the best source to farm for metal?

A. Fences

B. Lampposts

C. Vehicles

D. Shipping Containers

2. What is the ideal loadout balance?

A. 2 weapons : 2 healing items : 1 extra

B. 1 weapon : 3 healing items : 1 extra

C. 3 weapons : 1 healing items : 1 extra

D. 2 weapons : 3 healing items : 0 extra

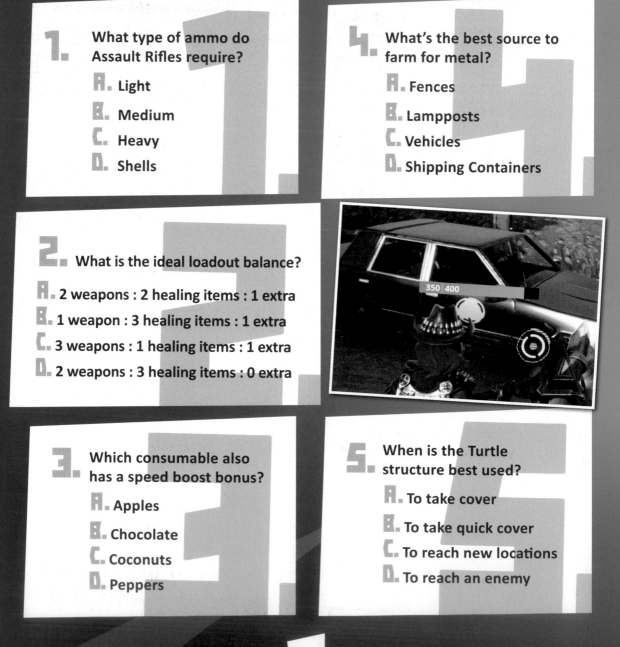

3. Which consumable also has a speed boost bonus?

A. Apples

B. Chocolate

C. Coconuts

D. Peppers

5. When is the Turtle structure best used?

A. To take cover

B. To take quick cover

C. To reach new locations

D. To reach an enemy

6. What weapon type is best for long distance?

A. Assault Rifles

B. Pistols

C. Sniper Rifles

D. Miniguns

7. What weapon type is best for up close and personal dueling?

A. Sniper Rifles

B. Shotguns

C. Launchers

D. SMGs

8. Which weapon type has the shortest range?

A. Launchers

B. Shotguns

C. SMGs

D. Assault Rifles

9. When taking damage, what healing item should you prioritise using?

A. Shield Potion

B. Bandages

C. Medkit

D. Slurp Juice

10. Which speedy method of travel allows you to use your weapons while on the go?

A. Gliders

B. Rift-to-Go

C. Zipline

D. Balloons

11. Which vehicle is best for smashing through an enemy's build?

A. Driftboard

B. Baller

C. Quadcrasher

D. None of the above

HOW TO EARN V BUCKS

PLAY BATTLE PASS CHALLENGES COMPETE LOCKER ITEM SHOP CAREER **STORE**   31 FPS [↓ 43 ↑ 60]

⏱ LIMITED TIME
OFFERS

V-BUCKS

	12% BONUS!	25% BONUS!	35% BONUS!	
1,000 V-BUCKS	**2,800** V-BUCKS	**5,000** V-BUCKS	**13,500** V-BUCKS	**THE WILDE PACK** + 600 V-BUCKS
$9.99	$24.99	$39.99	$99.99	$4.99

EARNING V BUCKS

While Fortnite: Battle Royale is Free-to-Play, it does have some optional purchases you can make to tailor your death island experience to your own particular tastes. The item shop allows you to buy countless custom cosmetics, but to do so, you'll need V-Bucks. These glowing coins will let you don a giant banana suit, swap your pickaxe for a candy cane or dance like that kid you saw on Ellen.

V-Bucks can be bought with real-world currency, but hold on – you don't have to crack open your wallet if you've got your heart set on that Beef Boss hamburger head (no judgment, no judgment). There are other ways in-game to earn the V-Bucks you need to get the cosmetic you so desire.

WARNING!

Never click on any links that promise free V-bucks. The only way to get V-bucks for free is to earn them via in-game activities and events. Countless scam sites try to prey on desperate gamers looking for a quick boost to buy a new cosmetic, promising endless V-Bucks in exchange for some details – every single one of these are fake, and may result in your account being stolen, as well as your personal information. That dance emote isn't worth your identity, pal. Stay vigilant.

WEIRD FLEX, BUT OKAY

Remember that V-Buck purchases are purely to flex – there's nothing you can buy that will give you a gameplay advantage. The developers have long been adamant about avoiding pay-to-win practices, and have always said that any in-game purchases are purely cosmetic.

WEEKLY BATTLE PASS CHALLENGES

The Battle Pass is an in-game system that provides gameplay challenges to the player and rewards. There's a Free Pass, but they only contain a limited amount of tasks compared to the full pass. The Battle Pass costs V-Bucks to acquire, but you can also earn them to make the purchase through the free challenges. You know what they say: you've got to spend a little money to make a little money, and Battle Pass more than returns its initial cost, as you can earn up to 25,000 V-Bucks with it in your possession.

The pass gives access to Weekly Challenges (including three free challenges), which can range from locating certain items or landmarks on the map, finding mushrooms in the forest or taking out a certain amount of enemies. The task switches up its ask every week, and keeps the Battle Royale shtick fresh as you go in with new challenges alongside the whole try-to-outlive-everyone-and-beat-the-storm gig.

Completing these weekly challenges also comes with a bonus, as you'll be given Battle Stars for your efforts. This will level up your Battle Pass, which allows you to climb the ranks. Climbing ranks doesn't come unrewarded; you can earn special cosmetics and fabled V-Bucks depending on the tier you reach.

FORTNITE: SAVE THE WORLD

The other free methods of earning V-Bucks are tied to Fortnite: Save the World, the PvE edition of Battle Royale. V-Bucks are shared across your account, so any money you earn in Save the World will be available to splash in Battle Royale.

> **Daily Logins:** This is by no means the fastest method of padding out your in-game wallet, but it's certainly the most dependable. Staying consistent with your daily logins will reward you with a variety of different bonuses every day, including the occasional V-Bucks drop.

> **Daily Quests:** Save the World gives you access to Daily Quests after you have advanced through the main storyline. These quests are similar tasks to the Battle Pass challenges from Battle Royale, but give you V-Bucks as a reward for completion.

> **Storm Shield Missions:** Storm Shield Missions take place in each of the four areas you unlock in the main storyline. Each area has 6 initial Storm Shield Missions, with 4 extra unlockable missions too. Completing these will yield you quite a healthy V-Buck drop.

> **Side Quests and Challenges:** Not all side quests are made equal, so not all promise V-Bucks, but there are certain ones that hand out up to 150 V-Bucks. You can also take on Challenges, which are unlocked at specific times, depending on your progress throughout the game. You can find these under the 'Quests' sub-menu.

LET'S DANCE

Fortnite is just as famous for its gameplay and constant content updates as it is for its in-game dance moves, and perhaps the latter even more so. Ask a non-gamer layman to accurately mime a Fortnite snipe shot and they may freeze, but there's a pretty strong chance they'd be able to pull off a convincing Fortnite floss.

Dancing in Fortnite is an art form in itself – selecting the perfect moves to bust out over the opponent you just unloaded a few shells into can be just as nuanced as deciding which weapon to take into the duel in the first place. A true Fortnite victor is well-versed in their Victory Royale dance repertoire from old school classics to viral sensations, but do you know the origins of the game's most popular emotes?

RIDE THE PONY

Remember when Gangnam Style was a thing? This emote is inspired by K-Pop star Psy's iconic horse riding dance from the viral mega-hit that was so strange, the whole world just had to watch it over three billion times.

BEST MATES

On the other end of the public conscious spectrum comes Best Mates, a dance inspired by a viral video uploaded by internet star Marlon Webb. The original featured Webb and his, well, best mates, using the loose-limbed move to meet up while wearing 80s workout gear and set to "Take on Me" by a-ha, naturally.

FRESH

This one's a classic, and better known in pop culture as 'the Carlton'. It was created by actor Alfonso Ribeiro as Carlton Banks in the 1990s sitcom The Fresh Prince of Bel-Air. Originally, it would be busted out if Tom Jones' "It's Not Unusual" was playing, but post-360-no-scope is also an appropriate condition these days.

FLOSS DANCE

This cursed creation was brought into the world by Russell Horning, AKA 'Backpack Kid'. Yes, the move has long had its multiple variations, but Backpack Kid's emotionless, dead-in-the-eyes expression while flossing with a backpack strapped to his back is really what catapulted it into popular culture.

GROOVE JAM

Vote for Pedro! Groove Jam is a throwback to the early 2000s as Napoleon Dynamite (played by Jon Heder) burned that canned heat in his heels on stage in front of his entire school at the class president rally.

JUBILATION

Now here's a throwback. Jubilation is a tribute to the old sitcom Seinfeld, which aired back in the 90s. It's a reference to Julia Louis-Dreyfus' character Elaine's iconic celebration.

ORANGE JUSTICE

And of course, Orange Justice – perhaps most iconic because it's a true Fortnite original. That's right: no references, no tributes; Orange Justice is 100% OG, and was actually created by a player.

Orange Shirt Kid (aptly named) first emerged in Epic's 2018 BoogieDown competition, where fans submitted videos of themselves dancing in hopes of seeing their moves added to the game. While Orange Shirt Kid didn't win the contest, overwhelming fan support prompted developers to add it anyway. Justice served.

FRIEND LIKE FORTNITE

When everything kicked off back in 2017, the Fortnite experience simply meant being dropped off on a cartoon-ish island, hoping to be the last out of 100 standing. But this year introduced more objectives and modes than ever, as 2019 saw Fortnite make some record-breaking collaborations with big, real-world names making their way into the game. Let's take a look at some of 2019's hallmark crossovers. Did you manage to catch any of these limited time events?

FORTNITE X MARSHMELLO

Fortnite partnered with popular EDM DJ Marshmello back in February 2019. It was the first of a tentative project called the Fortnite Concert Live series, where players could attend an exclusive (pre-recorded) concert ingame. Over 10.7 million players attended the virtual performance live in Pleasant Park, making it the game's biggest event day ever; and that's just counting those who logged in (the official recap video on YouTube has almost 40 million views).

FORTNITE X JORDAN

Here's one for the hypebeasts: 2019 saw the popular Jordans brand debut one of their shoe collections virtually. This collab had a heavy emphasis on cosmetics, with two new skins in signature Jordan colours and customizable Air Jordan 1s. It also included the Brooklyn-inspired skateboard-themed LTM Downtown Drop, which marked the first time Epic teamed up with community creators to develop official branded content.

FORTNITE X AVENGERS: ENDGAME

The Avengers: Endgame event was a follow-up from the super popular Infinity War collab, where players hunted for the Infinity Gauntlet to become Thanos and decimate everyone unfortunate enough to be on the same map. The End Game riff added a new team-based game mode where players could either wield iconic weapons from the Marvel universe or be part of Thanos' alien army.

FORTNITE X GODZILLA KING OF THE MONSTERS

In another major crossover with Hollywood, the king of the lizards made its debut in Fortnite this year. The collab was first teased with the POI in Polar Peak cracking, revealing a mammoth yellow eye encased within the ice that tracked the player's movements when approached.

FORTNITE X JOHN WICK

Everyone's favorite hitman came to Fortnite this Spring to promote the franchise's third installment. Players could participate in the LTM Wick's Bounty, and get two new John Wick skins, as well as cosmetics items. The collab was first teased by developers when players discovered a house belonging to the assassin in Paradise Palms before the update dropped.

45

FORTNITE CREATIVE

BUILD YOUR OWN FORTNITE! EVERYTHING YOU DO HERE IS SAVED.

While Battle Royale is undeniably a classic, sometimes dropping down from a balloon-buoyed bus to fight to the death can get a little… rinse-and-repeat. Thus came Season 7, with a brand new sandbox mode called Fortnite Creative.

Creative allows the player to create and design your own personal Battle Royale island to host your very own deathmatches, race modes, parkour obstacles courses, or anything your heart desires.

THE CREATIVE HUB

In Creative, you have access to your own island, your friends' islands, and selected featured islands from the community. The Creative hub world is filled with pillars and portals. You can access your own maps via the golden rift.

CREATIVE TIP #2

Wondering how the Quadcrasher handles? Just build a floor or staircase and add a vehicle spawner to take any vehicle you'd like for a spin around the island.

CREATIVE TIP #1

Creative is a great space to practice your building battles for the main Battle Royale mode. With infinite building materials, you won't have to worry about gathering all of them… or looking over your shoulder the whole time.

MY ISLANDS: THE BUILD

Everything on your island can be controlled by the AR Phone item in your inventory. This smart device can do anything from flipping a wall upside down or duplicating an infinite amount of refrigerators. You can use this to build your island to fit your exact specifications.

Populating a map may be a little intimidating, but you can start with some ready-made options. Pre-built structures and existing Fortnite assets (from the apartment blocks of Tilted Towers to the arctic test labs of Frosty Flights) can be found in the Prefabs sub menu.

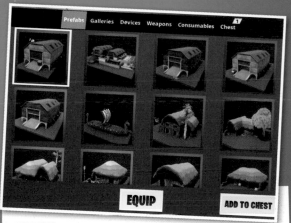

TIP!

Looking for somewhere to start? Prefabs can be super useful to unpick if you want bits and pieces for your own vision. The obstacle course is great for practice and parkour builds, and the Indestructible Gallery is useful to control player movement in deathmatches.

It will take a while to fully navigate your way around the building aspect of Creative since there's so many possibilities, and the best practice is really just to dive in and get familiar with everything on offer. However, there are some key skills you should work on finessing first before attempting a deep dive:

❯ To evenly space your items in an orderly fashion, you'll need to utilize the Grid Snap feature. You can activate this using the V key.

❯ To make objects float, toggle 'off' under the Drop option assigned to the G key. This will make the item hover in the air (which is great for parkour modes).

❯ To get around your map faster, double tap the space bar to fly.

MY ISLANDS: GAME MODES

With your build complete, it's now up to you to decide how exactly players can interact with your map. In My Island, you can customise the score presets, time limits, starting health and shields, respawn height, fall damage… anything you want to adjust is yours to alter. The world – or island, I suppose – is truly your oyster, and it would be impossible to cover all the possible options, so here are some popular ideas:

❭ **Practice Grounds:** Be sure to switch your Game Privacy to Private to allow yourself the privacy to stoat around your practice ground and test out some new or unfamiliar mechanics. If you want to practice duos or teams, you can invite up to 3 other players into Private islands.

❭ **Racing:** Race your friends to the finish line on a custom race track with a realism spectrum from Gran Turismo to Mario Kart – just how tied are you to the abiding the laws of gravity?

After you've built your desired track, hit the My Island tab from the ingame menu to set the race rules. You can customise anything from time limits, spawn location, gravity levels and build ability during play.

TIP!

Want to give an old classic a spin? Try Falconstrike1998's recreation of the iconic Rainbow Road from Super Mario Kart (Island Code: 2668-3299-2351).

❭ **Skate Parks:** You can make your very own skatepark to catch some air and grind some rails with your Driftboard. If the regular, old skate park is too 'classic' for you, why not try a life-threatening spin on things with a Driftboard-only deathrun?

Downtown Drop, the LTM for the Fortnite x Jordans crossover, was the first time a creative map was featured as a main-game LTM. The Brooklyn-inspired game mode was created by NotNellaf and Mollmolia.

OTHER ISLANDS

You can access islands created by other players in the hub world via the Island Codes system.

Island Codes are 12-digit strings unique to each created island. You can input these codes into rifts in the hub world to check out other players' works.

If you're curious and looking to trawl for some inspiration or a unique gameplay experience, you can find a bunch of different Island Codes online. The Fortnite Creative subreddit (r/FortniteCreative) is a great place to browse for places to visit, and online publications regularly post features including the codes to their favorite Creative discoveries.

FEATURED ISLANDS

If you're not looking for anything in particular, why not check out the Featured Islands? These builds have been hand-picked to feature as some of the best the community has to offer and is constantly being updated; experience anything from a team match across the ruins of Valhalla to a haunted pirate's deathrun.

Hey, and if you're feeling particularly proud of your own creation, you can submit your island to be included on the Featured Islands list on the official Epic Games website (as well as tips from the developers as to what they look for when reviewing submissions).

FROM YOUR ISLAND TO THE WORLD

Sometimes the Featured Islands list isn't big enough. A 16 player limit isn't enough. The creative audience just isn't enough. Ever dreamt of getting your own creations into the main game? Well, it's a tough ask, but it's not impossible.

The Forntite team introduced the LTM Creator Contest in Spring 2019, where they select a creator from the community to join the Support a Creator program and have their game mode featured as a fully-realized LTM, alongside Epic created modes like Team Rumble and 50v50.

The LTM Creator Contest only accepts submissions at specific competitive times. If you're looking for a year-round opportunity to have your creation appear in the main game, then the Block is for you.

THE BLOCK

So you've learnt the ropes over in Creative and you've made something you're proud to put your name on. 16 players seems a little meager... why not try for every single Battle Royale player across the world?

This is where the Block comes in: a flat 25x25 slab of concrete that replaced Risky Reels back at the end of 2018. Though its location has since moved, its purpose remains the same: a space to showcase the best of the creations built by players in the game's Creative mode.

SUBMITTING YOUR BUILD

Before you submit your build, you have to make sure it follows the guidelines that were set out by the Fortnite team:

❱ It must be a 25x25 tile area on a flat section of your island.

❱ It must be an original idea.

❱ Less is more; keep the Memory Used below 50,000.

❱ There's no height requirement/restriction, but try to keep it in line with existing POIs on the map.

❱ You can use any component available.

❱ Don't worry about vehicle, floor loot or chest spawns; they will be included by Epic.

Now, you may think your Block submission is the next coming of Tilted Towers, but it's important to remember the actual professional's (i.e., the game developers) words of advice when crafting your entry. The Fortnite Team have also stated that while reviewing Block submissions, they look for a unique aesthetic and level design, thoughtful set dressing, dynamic player pathing and significant landmarks other players can use for callouts.

Looming Llama by Stormhawk

Grimy Greens by kaancitak

THE BEST OF THE BLOCK 2019

Did you catch any of these creations while playing Battle Royale this year? There were countless creative iterations of the Block, but here are some of the highlights of 2019.

❯ **Grimy Greens by kaancitak:** The OG Block entry, a mysterious overgrown facility that set the stage for submissions to come.

❯ **Lunar Street Festival by NiBLL:** This themed creation was introduced to usher in the Lunar New Year.

❯ **Looming Llama by Stormhawk:** A mechanical monstrosity shaped like... a llama?

THINGS TO AVOID:

❯ Large, empty interiors

❯ Designs that reuse too many existing assets

❯ Designs that resemble old Battle Royale locations

❯ Zones that hinder player movement in fights

❯ Images, artwork, words or lyrics that are under copyright

For a full list of do's and don'ts from the Epic developers, check out the Creative Featured Content post on the official Fortnite site.

Once you're sure that your creation follows both the guidelines and Fortnite Creative's code of conduct, then you can submit it to be featured on the Block. Submissions can be made via a Google Doc on the official Fortnite site. Good luck!

FORTNITE WORLD CUP 2019

2019 was a banner year for Fortnite's presence in the esports scene, with a dogged dedication to cementing its place as a serious sporting event worldwide. Nothing quite sang that success like the very first Fortnite World Cup championship held at the end of July. Players from all around the globe flocked to the Arthur Ashe Stadium in New York City to compete in front of 23,000 fans for their share of a massive $30,000,000 (that's a lot of V-Bucks).

FORTNITE WORLD CUP FINALS

SOLOS

Over 40 million players competed for a chance to play in the solo Fortnite World Cup Finals, with 100 skilled players making it to the tournament in New York City. The lucky 100 played a series of six games to determine who would take home the title of the world's best, and it was clear from Game 1 that 16-year-old Kyle "Bugha" Giersdorf did not come to play (figuratively speaking, of course). Bugha dominated all six games with an early points lead, and won the $3,000,000 prize package in a very dominant showing.

Couldn't make it out to the arena? About six months too late? No worries, Epic has uploaded the broadcasts from the World Cup weekend on the official Fortnite YouTube channel. It's definitely worth a watch to see the world's best go toe-to-toe, shotgun-to-shotgun.

DUOS

The Duos tournament was held before the Solo rounds, with 50 of the best Duo teams playing across a series of six matches to see who had the best partnership in the game. America may have come up top in Solos, but it was Europe who took the Duo title, thanks to Emil "Nyhrox" Bergquist Pedersen and David "Aqua" W. They also won a cool $3,000,000.

WORLD CUP CREATIVE FINALS

The Creative Finals saw eight teams of four players compete for the title as Creative Champion across a series of challenges crafted in the game's Creative mode. Each squad was headed by a famous Fortnite streamer, with Cizzorz, Gotaga, Handofblood, Danyancat, Lachlan, Rubius, Tomoya and Mr. Fortnite himself, Ninja, leading their team into the fray. In the end, Fish Fam – led by Cizzorz – secured the win from a tight race, and won the biggest share of the prize pool: $1,345,000.

PRO-AM

It's not news to anyone that celebrities like to play Fortnite, and after several high-profile appearances from celebs across both streaming platforms and in the actual game itself, it only made sense that they would also make an appearance at the first world cup.

Pro AM saw 50 pro gamers pair up with 50 different celebrities to compete for a $3,000,000 prize pool – for charity, of course. Popular pairs included Ewok and actor Jordan Fischer, Wade.CN and Ninjaz dancer Jawn Ha, and Ninja and DJ Marshmello.

But none of the new pairings were a match for the tried-and-tested Airwaks and EDM producer RL Grime, the defending champions of the Pro-Am tournament. They took it home again in the World Cup Finals, earning $1,000,000 for their chosen charities.

TWO OUT OF FOUR ISN'T BAD

Despite being the "face of Forntite", pro player Tyler "Ninja" Blevins didn't qualify for the 2019 World Cup Solo or Duo finals. Of course, he still took part in the Pro-Am and Creative Finals. It's not a major Fortnite milestone without Ninja being there.

PRO-FILES: THE PRO STARS OF FORTNITE

Fortnite has a mammoth presence in the streaming world across a variety of platforms; check the game's category on Twitch and you'll find around 100,000 active viewers watching different channels at any one time.

Sometimes you've got to watch the best to be the best, and when it comes to Fortnite streamers, this selection is arguably the best of the best.

NINJA

DID YOU KNOW?

Ninja was the first PC player to reach the 5000 win milestone

Does this guy even need an introduction? Since the game's launch, Tyler "Ninja" Blevins has emerged as the face of the game, Mr. Fortnite himself, and one of the most popular Fortnite players on the planet.

Ninja's streaming career began in 2011, and he was one of the first to stream Fortnite regularly. On Twitch, he quickly rose to become the most followed streamer on the platform, boasting 11 million followers when he won Best Content Creator at the 2018 Game Awards. While he flourished on Twitch, he made a highly publicized exclusive move to Mixer in August 2019, where he hit 1 million subscribers just five days after the announcement.

WHERE TO WATCH:

❯ Mixer
❯ YouTube

DID YOU KNOW?

Ninja was the first PC player to reach the 5000 win milestone

TFUE

Turner "Tfue" Tenney is a huge name in Fortnite, with over 10 million subscribers on YouTube, 6 million on Twitch and 1.6 million on Twitter.

Like Ninja, he came to Fortnite with vast experience in older FPS games to build upon, and is widely considered to be one of the best competitive Fortnite players in the world. He has won the Korean Open 2019 with his partner KittyPlayers, and has consistently placed highly in various other competitive Fortnite events, earning over half a million US dollars in prize money alone.

WHERE TO WATCH:

❯ Twitch
❯ YouTube

BEST KNOWN FOR:
High skill, no nonsense play and consistent competitive success.

MYTH

Ali "Myth" Kabbani is a pro player that is widely known as one of (if not the) best builders in the game, and one of the first streamers to be picked up by a professional org.

He began streaming back in 2013, but really took off with the Fortnite release in 2017 – with only 800 subscribers pre-Fortnite, this number has sky-rocketed to 4 million today. He joined the esports organization Team SoloMid in 2018, and became captain of their Fortnite team. He is known as an entertainer, and often collaborates with other popular streamers across the Twitch platform, including his TSM teammates.

WHERE TO WATCH:

❯ Twitch
❯ YouTube

BEST KNOWN FOR:
Insane building skills and fun Fortnite event vlogs.

TIMTHE TATMAN

DAKOTAZ

Timothy "TimtheTatman" Betar is a popular streamer with a variety channel that attracts thousands of viewers every day. Though he is technically a variety streamer, his viewership skyrocketed with the release of Fortnite.

While he brings FPS skills and mechanics from games such as Overwatch and CS:GO to the table, he is best known as an entertainer. In 2018, he won the Fan Favorite Male Streamer of the Year at the Gamer's Choice Awards.

Brett "Dakotaz" Hoffman is a streamer best known for his insane sniping skills, as well as color commentary and elite gameplay.

Interestingly, Dakotaz is one of the very few popular streamers that does not stream with a face cam: the focus is solely on his gameplay, but he spices up his streams with in-depth commentary and lots of interaction with his chat. Watch Dakotaz's streams to witness his frightening sniper precision, and learn about sniping details, like opponent movement prediction and judging bullet drops.

WHERE TO WATCH:

❱ Twitch
❱ YouTube

WHERE TO WATCH:

❱ Twitch
❱ YouTube

BEST KNOWN FOR:

The perfect blend of top skill and top entertainment.

BEST KNOWN FOR:

In-depth commentary, no facecam and lots of interaction with his community.

SYPHERPK

Ali "SypherPK" Hassan is a member of the popular esports org Luminosity. His fanbase is called the SypherHood.

Like all streamers, SypherPK has great skill, but what makes him a must watch is his focus on educational content, like his 'How to Win' series on YouTube. His streams are also great to learn from, as he often dedicates slots of time to fine-tuning mechanical practice, and is well-known in the community for his great trap eliminations.

WHERE TO WATCH:

❯ Twitch

❯ YouTube

BEST KNOWN FOR:
Educational gameplay videos and fun collaborations.

NICKMERCS

While the vast majority of pros pick the PC as their platform of choice, Nick "NICKMERCS" Kolcheff is one of the best console players out there.

Though he does stream often on Twitch, his most valuable knowledge base is housed on his YouTube channel, which he updates with stream highlights and educational content every day. He also often creates fun in-game challenges, like Hand Cannon-only victories, or his No Materials challenge.

WHERE TO WATCH:

❯ Twitch

❯ YouTube

BEST KNOWN FOR:
High-level console gameplay and interesting challenges.

FORTY FORTNITE FACTS YOU DIDN'T KNOW

❱ Fortnite is developed by Epic Games, the team behind Unreal Tournament, Gears of War and Infinity Blade.

❱ The game is developed on Unreal Engine 4.

❱ Fortnite is named after the British phrase 'fortnight'. This is taken from the hardest mode in the main game, where a player has to survive for two weeks against a slew of zombies.

❱ The game's genre - battle royale - is inspired by the famous Japanese novel (and subsequent movie adaptation) 'Battle Royale' by Koushun Takami.

❱ The game's original art style was a lot darker and creepier than what we know now, but tester feedback prompted the design team to change directions...

❱ ...The game already featured a doomsday vibe and zombies, and they didn't want Fortnite to be categorised as a horror game alongside the likes of DayZ...

❱ ...So the team went for a brighter, more cartoonish aesthetic inspired by Pixar, Tim Burton and Looney Tunes.

❱ Why those three? Because they wanted to appeal to players of all ages, so they took inspiration from popular animations from different generations.

❱ Epic first announced Fortnite back in 2011. A rocky road to development eventually saw the game release in 2017...

❱ ...but it's still in Early Access, which technically means it hasn't been officially released yet.

❱ The Battle Royale mode that took the world by storm isn't even the main game; it was a special mode developed as special mode within the huge, PVE story-driven game: Save the World.

❱ In fact, the Battle Royale mode was originally an experiment. The decision to release Battle Royale separately was made just two weeks before the projected launch date.

❱ The Battle Royale mode is credited by many as "saving" the game. On its launch day, it had over 1 million players, and has grown steadily since.

❱ After its first month, the game had shifted over 500,000 digital copies.

❱ In fact, the game almost grew too popular. In February 2018, it reached a peak of 3.4 million concurrent players, which caused a service outage.

❱ The incident was unprecedented, and prompted Epic to post a plea for help on their website for anyone with domain expertise to help them scale the game to match its meteoric growth.

❱ The game is now so popular it is truly a pop culture titan. Fortnite made more money in April 2018 than 'Avengers: Infinity War' did on its opening weekend.

❱ And Fortnite now has more users worldwide than Netflix.

❱ When EA launched their own battle royale game, Apex Legends, it was billed as the "Fortnite Killer". Fortnite still reigns supreme.

❱ Fortnite is the most viewed game on Twitch.

❱ Battle Royale has remained Free-to-Play since its release. The producers stated that they have always tried to avoid 'Pay to Win' traps that may alienate the player base, which is why they only have cosmetics available to purchase.

❱ Despite interest, Epic has stated that they have no plans to develop a first-person mode to the game.

❱ The game is available on almost the full range of gaming platforms: PS4, Xbox One, Nintendo Switch, PC, Mac and mobile.

❱ Fortnite was one of the first games to majorly promote cross-play, which means you can dance ontop of your best friend's corpse no matter what they're playing on.

❱ Fortnite has a booming esports scene that really took off with its first ever world cup in April, 2019.

❱ ...They also run a special tournament for celebrities, who duo up with pro players. Joel McHale, Marshmellow and Lil Yachty all took part in the inaugural season.

❱ The game has become so popular that Epic had to dedicate a specific workforce to work exclusively on Fortnite...

❱ ...Which has led some blame Fortnite's success for the closure of other Epic titles, like Paragon.

❱ But the competitive nature of Fortnite has brought out the worst in some. In their ongoing battle against hackers, Epic Games famously took a 14-year old cheater to court.

❱ All of the island's locations are named with alliteration. Haunted Hills, Sunny Steps, Lonely Lodge... can't unsee it now, huh?

❱ Each of the map's quadrants takes 45 seconds to cross on foot.

❱ The Moai heads found across the map are randomly generated, and they are based on the monolithic statues from Easter Island.

❱ There's a secret supervillain base hidden in the mountain of Snobby Shores, the perfect spot to hatch plans against...

❱ ...the superhero that clearly lives in the Wayne Manor-esque mansion in Lonely Lodge, complete with a hi-tech cave in the basement.

❱ Have you ever wondered where exactly it is that everyone loads in while waiting for the game to start? You can spot Spawn Island South West of the main map when you're deploying from the Battle Bus. You can't access it, but you can still see it in the distance.

❱ Best get familiar with the current map, because a new one isn't coming any time soon. The lead level designer stated that they won't move onto a new map until the current one fails to reach the needs of the players.

❱ The Zapatron was so powerful that it had to be removed from the game. The devastating sniper rifle could one-shot an opponent by unleashing a stream of electricity.

❱ The Crossbow was another weapon that got vaulted for being too overpowered, but unlike the Zapatron, the Crossbow still makes the odd comeback for special events.

❱ Due to a Tweet challenge, an Ohio high school chemistry teacher had to write all of the finale exam questions in relation to Fortnite. The challenge was to reach 6,700 retweets; it finished with over 30,000.

❱ Fortnite's creator, Tim Sweeney, is one of the largest landowners in North Carolina. He buys the land to preserve the state's wilderness. Now you know where your V-Bucks are going.

FORTNITE IN NUMBERS

Fortnite has seen unparalleled success since its launch, but in the last few years, it has also managed to become a record-breaking phenomenon of which we've never truly seen before. Sure, it's a popular game with a lot of pop culture relevance, but did you know quite how big of a mark the game has made in the record books?

MOST VIEWED STREAM

What do you get when you mix the world's most popular game, Twitch's most popular streamer and one of the biggest rappers in the world? New records, for sure.

In 2018, Drake tweeted that he would be playing Fortnite on Twitch with the platform's biggest streamer, Ninja, as well as NFL rookie JuJu Smith-Schuster and rapper Travis Scott. At its peak, their squad stream brought in **628,000** concurrent viewers, which smashed the previous 388,000 viewers for a single-player stream record to smithereens.

HIGHEST GROSSING VIDEO GAME

While Fortnite is free-to-play, the game still manages to rake in record amounts of money, making it the highest grossing game of all time. The game made **$323,000,000** (USD) in May 2018 – the biggest month ever for a video game. The State of Screens report found that Fortnite had managed to outgross numerous successful Hollywood blockbusters, including Jumanji: Welcome to the Jungle, Wonder Woman and even Spider-Man: Homecoming.

In that record-breaking month of May, a cumulative total of **2.7 billion** hours of Fortnite were played worldwide - that's over **300,000** years.

THE MOST POPULAR VIDEO GAME

Yes, it's easy to say Fortnite is the most popular video game in the world when even your grandparents have probably heard of it, but the game actually has the numbers to back up such grand claims. There are reportedly over **250 million** Fortnite users worldwide, which is more than three times larger than the UK population, and over two thirds of the US population.

BIGGEST IN-GAME CONCERT

DJ Marshmello has had many ties with the world of Fortnite, but perhaps none as monumental as the record-breaking concert he held in-game, making it the most attended concert in history... technically. The in-game event was Fortnite's first concert, and boasted a reported attendance of over **10 million** players.

Make EDM, Not War: In order to ensure everyone could enjoy the concert without worries of a rogue rocket launcher on the loose, Epic disabled everyone's ability to wield weapons for the duration of the show.

BIGGEST WORLD CHAMPION PRIZE

Epic Games invested a lot of money into esports in 2019, and showcased the pinnacle of their efforts at the 2019 Fortnite World Cup. The top prize for the Solo and Duo rounds was a whopping **$3,000,000** (USD), which – for perspective – is higher than the top prizes for the Indy 500, Tour de France and even Wimbledon.

QUIZ ANSWERS

Check your answers from the survival quiz (p. 38 – 39) and add up your total score to find out where you place in the true Battle Royale: game knowledge.

1. A – 0, B – 3, C – 1, D – 0
2. A – 3, B – 1, C – 2, D – 0
3. A – 0, B – -1, C – 0, D – 3
4. A – 2, B – 0, C – 3, D – 1
5. A – 3, B – 1, C – 0, C – 0
6. A – 2, B – 1, C – 3, D – 0
7. A – 0, B – 3, C – 1, D – 2
8. A – 0, B – 2, C – 3, D – 1
9. A – 3, B – 2, C – 1, D – 0
10. A – 0, B – 0, C – 3, D – 0
11. A – 0, B – 2, C – 3, D – 0

RESULTS

0-9 POINTS: YOU PLACED #100 - #75

Well, well... You'll be lucky if you make it off the bus, to be frank. The fundamentals aren't quite there yet, so you'd be best reading over the material again before leaping into battle.

10-18 POINTS: YOU PLACED #74 - #50

Not bad, not bad. You have a basic knowledge of the game and will likely be able to survive the landing rush, but you'll likely falter later in game when you start to come face to face with opponents and they out-maneuver you in 1v1s. Take a quick refresher on weapon efficiencies and healing item priorities, and you'll be able to make it even further.

19-27 POINTS: YOU PLACED #49 - #25

You're almost there! You definitely know enough to survive the scrimmage that is landing, you can make your way around the map well enough and know the basics of duels. At this point, it seems like the little details are eluding you, and might cost you that Top 25 placement. The finer points to the game will come with practice, so keep at it.

28-33 POINTS: YOU PLACED TOP 25!

Congratulations, Battle Royale Valedictorian. How does it feel to be so deadly? You've got the knowledge you need to make your way across the map and handle any altercation or obstacle you come across with quick efficiency and ease. All that stands in your way are other players with the same prowess. Practice will always give you the edge, so while you have the knowledge, don't be afraid to review, reinforce and experiment in Creative to keep you at the top of your game.

Victory Royale is certainly within your grasp. Got your dance emote of choice ready?